UTTER NONSENSE

The poems of PETER MORTIMER

For John
All Best Wishes

17.6.88

Illustrated by GEOFF LAWS

IRON PRESS

PETER MORTIMER (centre) was born in Nottingham, December 1943 after which Hitler soon gave up. The only visiting supporter at the Rochdale v Notts Co. Div 1V game (1961), and still cherishing the meat and potato pie, he now lives in the North-East coastal village of Cullercoats, an avid reader of the Beaufort scale and supporter of twice-daily tides. Four slim volumes of verse have appeared, plus five stage plays, & itinerant journalism. The editing of IRON press and magazine has prematurely greyed certain protuberances but failed to produce teevee advertising offers for sherry.

Geoff Laws (left) although an award-winning cartoonist, believes it may still be necessary to cut off at least part of an ear in order to achieve true greatness.

Until then he continues to work as the editorial artist for the Thomson Newspapers in Newcastle upon Tyne, where the canteen food has recently shown distinct improvement.

Contents

This edition first published 1986 by IRON Press
5 Marden Terrace, Cullercoats, North Shields
Tyne & Wear NE30 4PD. Tel: Tyneside (091)
2531901

Earlier editions of this book appeared in;
1977, 1978, 1979

ISBN 0 906228 27 1

Since first publication, many of the original
poems have been placed in anthologies in the UK and USSR. Of the new
work, *Bald Bertie* was first published by Macmillan
Education Ltd, *Oh Dear* by Platform Poets

The front cover is a rare drawing of a hedonistic
woof pig

Printed by Tyneside Free Press Workshop. Poems set in
12pt Sabon by True North. Cover by Geoff Laws
Book design by Norman Davison

Trade distribution;
Passsword (Books) Ltd
25 Horsell Rd
London
N1 1XL
01-607-1154

Foreword

It is now nine years since Messrs Mortimer & Laws invited me to write a foreword for the first edition of *Utter Nonsense* – an honour, and an all-too-rare communication for an individual cast in obscurity.

Those years have seen the further decline of my own intellectual standing, my removal from society has become more severe, my books publicly derided by such as Professor Orle de Quork, the Oxford collarist, and a sense of oblivion take hold.

All of which matters little. I have my small rom with its tiny metal window. I breathe the air. I eat the dust. Where then slavery? Smuggled inside my once-daily, lightly boiled egg I discover the same written request from Messrs Mortimer & Laws. They wish me well! They would (were it only possible) send me a lemon cream sandwich! Their book is to go to a fourth, and expanded edition. Can I once more put pen to paper?

Too kind. Here, I am armed merely with a stunted and well-chewed HB pencil, and an old pack of Rizla greens. It will suffice, and I recall those brave, albeit wretched souls, writers incarcerated for their visions, and forced to record their valued thoughts via a series of painful thigh lacerations. The red blood of truth!

I set to. I write, and smuggle out the sentences individually, one per Rizla paper. Being myopic, the warder scarcely gives a glance at his trouser turnup, nor the scribbled literature I secrete therein. I refresh myself on the book's original characters; Bigtrousers Dan, Gladys the Tadpole, Rogbog, Mr. Humpling the Dumpling. Via the egg I am informed of the newcomers – Bald Bertie, Nigel Newlywed, Bumless Norman.....

Beyond my four walls, I know the world increasingly prepares itself for an *auto da fe par excellence* (my passions will perhaps excuse the linguistic cocktail), and I can think only of the words from Gladys the Tadpole *"put down your guns, eat ice-cream and jelly"*. Why are our poets ever ignored? Does society learn nothing from the false ambition of Rogbog, the unwise scientific tamperings of Hubroil, Albertt's perpetual spontaneous combustion?

I offer you a hero; Bigtrousers Dan, inventor of a machine which manufactures only happiness. But I am rapidly tired by matters writing. With the companionship of only this seed drill and a 1935 Wisden, my energy levels decrease. Where now the days of the quadrangle greasepole marathons, the nightlong discurses of Schwitter? My dear friends are all long gone; brand managers with Tescos, Lloyds investment consultants.

When forewording the book in 1977 I wrote that it was "a form of art to which I raise my tattered flag". The pennant today is yet more decayed, a weakly fluttering rag. Not waving. But.

I take heart from the new book which I may never see. I am allowed the occasional McVities chocolate digestive (milk), a Ludo flurry *de temps en temps*. All literature is considered subversive. Daily I devour eagerly the faded wall scratchings of my predecessors, "wazza wuz ere" etc.

My friends, out there, enjoy this book. Read the poems well. Study the illustrations carefully. Be joyful that they are released into the world, where they belong. Aaarp! Aaarp! Aaarp!

Carl Zubrevsky
February 1986

For Mo and Dylan

Bald Bertie

Bertie was bald, as bald as can be
bald as a light bulb or a freshly shelled pea
as he walked down the street, the kids yelled "Mister!"
"How come yer bonce looks just like a blister?"

Chorus (Vivace)

Oh! Oh! Bertie!
And still not thirty!

He applied several lotions, he massaged in cream
he dolloped on potions – by the ton (was *he* keen!)
In a trim-fit wig, revved his new sports coupee
Went too fast with a girl, and off flew his toupee

Chorus

Oh! Oh! Bertie!....(etc.)

Spoke to doctors, answered adverts, (alas, none the wiser)
Sweated hours in a greenhouse, smeared his nut with fertiliser
Wrote as "Anxious, Bognor Regis", seeking help from *'Dear Diane'*
thumped his hairy dog called Norman. Grew quite desperate (like Dan)

Chorus

Oh! Oh! Bertie!...(etc)

Until one day he vanished with no forwarding address
Left one sock and well-worn toothbrush, a bed that was a mess
some say that he's in heaven, or very soon will be
but who's that lonely figure in the tight-fitting trilby?

Chorus

Oh! Oh! Bertie!

Hurray for the Waddle Fish

When the waddle fish came out of the sea
one hundred people said 'oh my, oh me'.
The Mayor took his hat off and stood on his head.
The Town Clerk didn't.
(Why?)
He stayed in bed.
Over the beach and onto the road
came the waddle fish, and was HE like a toad!
(No).
He didn't want popcorn or butter and toast
and rhubarb and custard he didn't want most
of all
Between you and me I think he was clever
to make all those people think, 'well, I never!'

Janitor Jeffries

Janitor Jeffries
bucket & mops
scrub
polish
wipe
never stops

Janitor Jeffries
cleaning the stair
tiles
steps &
window
in long underwear

Janitor Jeffries
up before dawn
wheeze
cough &
splutter
expression forlorn

Janitor Jeffries
bike in the rain
hills
puddles
splash
'gain and again

Janitor Jeffries
August arrives
your marks,
steady
go!
two weeks in St. Ives

Janitor Jeffries
feet in the sea
ice
cream &
winkles
o golly o me

Janitor Jeffries
a fortnight's delight
case
hat &
tickets
back Sunday night

Janitor Jeffries
bucket & mops
scrub
polish
wipe
never stops.

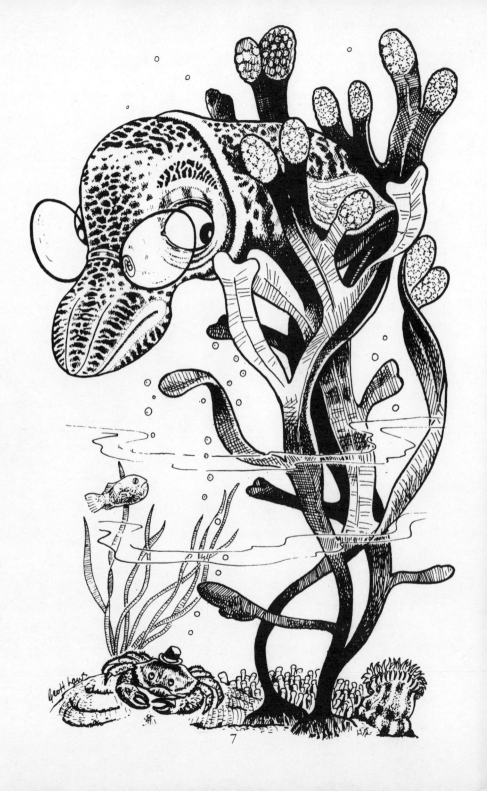

Herbert the Trouserless Squid

And o how he hid,
Herbert the trouserless squid.
Blushing he was
and rushing he was
and into the seaweed pushing he was
Embarrassed he was
and harrassed he was.
O was he red!
'My name
is shame!'
he said.
Looked for some breeks he did,
three long weeks he did.
No trousers to wear,
totally bare.
Looking for a tailor he was,
but caught by a sailor he was.
Now he's dressed he is.
Dressed for the best he is.
Caviar and wine sauce,
Herbert's the main course.
He is.

Exploding Albertt

Exploding Albertt
came into the room.
Boom, boom, boom,
BOOM! BOOM! BOOM!
He munched on a grape
and licked a meringue,
Bang, bang, bang,
BANG! BANG! BINGUE!
On the third of the month
and every wet Friday
Albertt exploded,
but he was neat and tidy.
'Oh dear and oh gosh'
he'd exclaim with a blush.
'I've gone all to pieces,
please pass me a brush'.
He'd sweep himself up
and replace every bit;
he'd stick them on tight
to make sure that they'd fit.

Our Albertt was puzzled,
he scratched at his head.
'Why can't I explode
on a Thursday instead?
Or the fourth of the month,
or when it's not raining?'
No-one could tell him,
there seemed no explaining.
Boom, boom went our Albertt,
boom boom, and crash wallop,
his limbs flew in the air
and came down in a dollop.

He exploded so much
(Oh much more than before!)
he blew off the roof,
one window and a door.
'I'm shocked, I'm amazed'
said his auntie called Hortense.
'This time it's too much,
you should really have more sense'.
Albertt checked in his diary,
(he was playing a hunch),
it was wet. It was Friday,
AND the third of the month.
'That explains it'
boomed Albertt.

11

Bigtrousers Dan

In the land of Rumplydoodle
where men eat jollips for tea,
and the cows in the hay
feel sleepy all day,
there's a wonderful sight to see.
On the banks of the River Bongbong,
in a hut made of turnips and cream,
sits a whiskery man,
name of Bigtrousers Dan,
and he plays with his brand new machine.
There are gronfles
and nogglets
and pluffles
and valves that go
ker-pling and ker-plang,
and a big sugar wheel
that revolves with a squeal
'till it's oiled with a chocolate meringue.
There are wurdlies
and flumdings
and crumchies
that go round just as fast as they can,
and a big chocolate ball
that makes no sound at all,
thanks to clever old
Bigtrousers Dan.

Mister Humpling the Dumpling's Coat

Mister Humpling the Dumpling took his coat to the cleaners.
He went back to collect it; the man said 'I've been as
helpful as I can, but the coat's covered in jelly'.
Thought Mister Humpling the Dumpling: 'That's all very well'. He
took it back home, and scrubbed it with water,
it wouldn't come clean, so he thought that he oughtta
take it abroad to a fat prince or a Rajah,
show it a captain, a corporal, a sarge, a
colonel, a major, or some distant ruler,
but nobody listened. They said 'don't be a fool, the
coat's gone all soggy, it's old and it's mouldy'.
Mister Humpling grew sad; with no coat he felt cold. He
wandered about, and got his feet wet in rivers,
he sneezed and he snuffled, and he moaned and said: 'Give us
a coat, my nose has gone blue, and hear my teeth chatter,
oh give us a coat, a hot drink, a warm hat, a
gas fire and some mustard, a mug of hot liquor,
don't let me grow cold, don't let me grow sick.' A
long time he wandered, 'till one day in the mountain,
he found an old castle with thick walls and a Count in.
'Come in' said the Count: 'You are blue, thin, and frozen,
you have ice in your hair, frost on your toes and
you need a nice coat, stewed prunes and suet pudding,
but please wipe your feet, and don't bring the mud in.'
So Mister Humpling got warm, then to his mother he wrote:
'I am living in a castle. There's no jelly on my coat.'

Miss Wobblegob Suet

Alak and alas for Miss Wobblegob Suet.
She's jumped from a 'plane.
(Said she would do it).
And never did ask what a parachute was.
Never did ask, and the reason's because
only that week Miss Wobblegob had seen
a man bounce in the air from a trampoline.
And there right away she thought men could fly,
and went rushing right off to jump from the sky.
But now, poor Miss Wobblegob's falling in flight
and beginning to think that something ain't right.
Lucky for her, there's a lot to be said
for falling five miles, and landing in bed.
(only dreaming, you see).

16

Great Carrot's Escape from the Munchers

Men with long noses and some gentlemen of worth
joined in the hunt when it sprang from the earth.
Men who cackled like geese and screeched like a parrot
took to the roads at the escape of Great Carrot.

Great Carrot woke up with a huge yawning sound,
combed its green hair and took a good look around.
It rustled its roots, then it shoved and it squeezed.
And soon it was free. My, my, was it pleased!

It looked north, it looked south, it looked east and then westerly,
but just couldn't decide which route would be besterly.
so it trundled away, oh so big, red and fat,
'till it came o the road and thought: 'Well, what is **that**?'

'I don't think I like it' thought Great Carrot sad and glum,
as it stood by the road, and watched the cars vroom, vroom, vroom.
Into his ear whispered the Vegetable Fairy:
'Go seek out King Beetroot'. And Carrot thought, 'dare he?'

He dared and he did, and went six to the dozen
to the land of King Beetroot, (who lived with his cousin).
To the land where a notice – oh – ever so wide
said 'No vegetable here shall be boiled baked or fried'.

Where the turnips looked happy, and the swedes were delirious.
Carrot leapt in the air, (things weren't quite so serious).
He danced on his head, and kissed a sweet pea.
Then bowed to the King (who was having his tea).

In the land of the Munchers, they'd begun a search party,
with ten men quite thin, and ten hale and hearty.
They had nets, they had spears, sharp knives and stew pot.
They wanted Great Carrot; sliced up sizzling hot!

They looked under stones, round corners, and in jellies,
they jumped into dustbins, baby cots & rubber wellies.
They grew hot red and angry, thumped the ground in despair.
'We've lost our Great Carrot. BOO HOO! It's not fair!'

For ten years they looked, then 100 years after.
And each year they felt, dafter dafter and dafter.
They all grew long beards, bent backs, and curly noses,
bald heads and carbuncles, and hair on their toeses.

In the land of King Beetroot by a gooseberry bush,
sits a smiling Great Carrot, but quiet please – hush!
He's snoozing and snoring, and feeling quite dozy.
Even a carrot can find out that life's rosy.

Herbert K.W. Tree

Herbert K.W. Tree
set all the animals free:
Unlocked the cages
(and it didn't take ages)
right there in the zoo.
Look here you,
said a fat-nosed judge,
this just won't do,
you can't do that,
I'll tell you flat.
And he banged on the table,
not very nice,
said now I am able
to punish you,
I'll do it in a thrice.
Locked him up
and he couldn't get out.
Teach you a lesson
said the judge with the snout.
But it didn't.

RogBog *the Pig Charmer*

With a stare and a song and a wave and a blink
Rogbog the Clever could make his pig think
that it wasn't a pig, no not a pig at all,
but something quite different, like a hat or a ball.

He could make his pig look like a great bowl of stew,
make it jump in the air like a fat kangaroo.
With a twirl of his fingers he could make it conjecture
the likelyhood of becoming a movie projector.

Nobody knew how Rogbog could do it,
even magicians said 'We haven't a clue, it
seems so amazing, can it truly be thus?'
Rogbog just smiled. Pig miaaawoed like a puss.

'Tell us your secret' said the folks 'We feel thwarted'.
'No' said Rogbog. The pig sat and snorted,
it danced on its nose, its head and its belly,
it jigged and it hopped, and it wobbled like jelly.

Alas for poor Rogbog, he took things too far.
In grabbing the pig, one day he said 'Ah!'
He stared and he sang and he waved and he blinked,
and said to the pig: 'I'll make you something extinct!'

'At the count of fourteen, and not one second more,
my pig will believe it's a huge dinosaur.
I'll shock and amaze you, it's my best trick to date.'
The crowd jumped to its feet (they just couldn't wait).

1, 2, 3, 4, 5, 6, 7, 8, 9, 10, 11, 12, 13, 14........

The pig made a roar and began gnashing its teeth;
it rose up in the air with the crowd down beneath.
It gobbled and munched and its ears went flip-flap,
its tail thumped the ground, and it buried a cat.

'Oh dear!' cried Rogbog and he felt his knees tremble
'I never quite thought you would so much resemble
a big slimy monster, please stop it and be
a fat hairy pig again, all soft and cuddly!'

Rogbog was too late, too late by a minute,
the people had fled, and left him there in it.
Munch munch went the pig, munch munch and slurp slurp,
it took a big swallow and let out a burp.

And ever since then, there's nobody wants to
meet up with the pig that thinks it's a monster.
They're shouting for Rogbog, and they're sounding so glum.
But they're shouting in vain, 'cos he's in the pig's tum.

Nigel Newlywed

Nigel Newlywed
took his brand new wife to bed
Oh – that black and shiny hair!
Those rose-red lips and skin so fair!
As for spots – they just weren't there.

(Nigel had come, so calm and cool
to snatch her free of the typing pool)

Thought he; now I do possess her
(like a Volvo – or welsh dresser)
In his yellow striped pyjamas
he felt about as calm as
a dog sat on a nettle
live lobster boiling in a kettle
a dancer, one leg shorter
than the other
("Help – I'm limping mother!")

Listen. Nigel's knees knock like maracas
I fear he's going crackers
Casts off a nylon sock
And scarce can stand the shock
of that milk-white rising bosom
But what's this?
"Er – there was – mmm –
just one thing, I fear
I should mention first my dear . . ."

"My sweetmeat my precious
my flower my darling
my scrumptious my dreamboat
my petal my doll

my delight my sugar
my cherry pie apple of my eye"

(how incredible
he should think her so edible)

"Just there, by your dainty ankle
my very own spouse
is a teeny-weeny
itsy-bitsy
oh so tiny
mouse"
"Aaaaaaaaaaaeeeeeeeeeeeoooooooowwww!"

Is it so surprizon
she was soon beyond the horizon?
Smiled Nigel/
poor poor poor poor poor thing
she'll be back soon, for me
and for the ring.

TIME PASSES

Satellites go to Mars
Ford invent new colours for cars
Vicars munch micro-wave pasties
while digesting video nasties
And Nigel/
counts the fluff in his belly but
wonders why he's still celibate
Poor poor poor poor poor thing
(he's still got the ring)

To her own little pillow
In her own little house
A girl whispers nightly
Thank you little mouse

Bum

Everyone has got a bum
From Nantwich to Peru
Lumberjacks, real docs (and quacks)
Her Royal Highness too

Sweaty wrestlers, scribbling clerks
Jailbirds with tattoed tum
Pale communists, girls rarely kissed
Each one has got a bum

Barbers, bankrupts, one-eyed toffs
New orphans rendered mumless
Large ballerinas, red-faced conveners
Just show me *one* who's bumless

Apart from Norman

Bumless Norman, Bumless Norman
Legs from his neck down to the floor, man
Safe job, warm house, jam tarts with his mum
No bum

He'd suffer the plague, bad breath, lumpy spuds
Confess Hitler was his finest chum
Any sacrifice (not just once, but twice)
If he wasn't, minus bum

Norman's glum

Gladys the Tadpole

This is the tale of a tadpole called Gladys,
who grew up all wrong, (and you know how bad that is).
Life in the pond found her fed-up and yawning,
while all her young friends were busy frog-spawning.

'I want to be a tiger, an elk or ant-eater'
said Gladys the tadpole, 'life could be sweeter
as a gnu or a buzzard, a giraffe or warthog,
anything I'll be but a fat slimy frog.

So she packed up a bag, and she took to the roads,
away from the lands of the green croaking toads.
She travelled afar, and wore a black floppy hat;
green braces and socks, striped shoes and cravatte.

She learnt how to bark, how to growl, and say 'woof!'
She bought four wooden legs, but still not enough.
She took lessons in fighting, and climbing up trees.
'Let me not be a frog!' said Gladys. 'Oh please!'

'Go back to your pond' said a wise hippo called Doris:
'You know there's no place for tadpoles in the forest.
Tadpoles don't fight, build nests or look growly,
they don't play silly games, monthly, daily, or hourly.

Gladys wouldn't listen, this talk did affront her,
until into the forest came stalking the White Hunter.
Lassoed her legs, locked her up, and what's worse is,
took her back home to be the star of the circus.

Poor, poor old Gladys, with her false stripes and fur:
A tadpole gone wrong, what an awful affair!
Now the circus crowds laugh, the audience is joking,
while she leaps through the hoop, (At the same time croaking).

The moral of the tale is easy to spot,
tadpoles should be happy with what they have got.
And white hunters too, even those on the tele,
should put down their guns, eat ice-cream and jelly.

The King and the Hatter

There once was a King
who'd never worn hats.
I know what you'll say,
'Just fancy that(s)!
One day in his court,
he thought,
perhaps I just ought.
So he picked up the 'phone
and rang up a hatter,
who wouldn't come at all.

'Oh well' said the King,
'it doesn't really matter'.

The Woof Pig

If you listen hard enough, enough,
you can hear a pig go woof, woof, woof.
Not all the time, just now and then.
There! Was that one?
No. Wrong again.

Babies are Boring

Babies are boring
(Oh yes they are!)
Don't believe mothers
or a doting papa.
Babies are boring,
their hands and their bellies,
their pink puffy faces
which wobble like jellies.
Accountants and grandmas
and sailors from Chile
when faced with a baby
act extraordinarily silly.
They grimace and they giggle,
say 'diddle-dum-doo',
they waggle their fingers
(stick their tongues out too).
They slaver and slurp
then they tickle its tummy
they gurgle and drool:
'Oh, he's just like his mummy!'
'Oh, his mouth is like Herbert's!'
'He's got Uncle Fred's nose!'
'My word, he looks healthy!'
'It's his feed, I suppose?'
Save me from baldness
and the old smell of kippers,
but most of all save me
from all gooey nippers.
I'm a brute, I'm a fiend
and no use to implore me
to tickle its chin,
because all babies bore me.

Hubroil's Strategic Error

He swallowed the pill
and then felt quite ill.
He should really have read
the label which said:
'All things may follow
if these pills you swallow.
The results will be
most alarming to see'.
And alarming they were,
Hubroil smelt like a sewer.
He grew fat as a toad,
then as long as a road,
he grew a nose big and hairy,
then wide wings like a fairy.
His skin turned bright blue,
his mouth said 'moo, moo!'
He flew up in the air,
and then growled like a bear.
His hair went corroded
then both legs exploded.
His arms floated away.
His head went the same way!
He bounced off the ground,
and went quite green and round,
until soon he was looking
like an apple for cooking.
'That'll do for me pie'
said a dame who passed by.
And with no further thought,
poor Hubroil was caught.
Sliced up in a pot
and cooked (oh so hot).
He's under the pastry
for acting so hasty.

Oh Dear

the government transferred the sea today
said a man in a hat "we'll take it away
the seaside's for all, and not just you few
we'll take it inland, and let them have a view".

so now it's all gone, and to fill up the space
they've put factories and flats all over the place
they've pulled down the piers and wrapped up the sand
and put it in lorries which hurried inland

in Sheffield and Leeds they're jumping for joy
at the smell of the briny, the sight of a buoy
and dirty black miners come up for a dip
where once it took hours on a coach tour day trip

said Mrs McGrumble who runs a sweet shop
"when they brought in the sea, it was quite a shock
but the man in the hat soon banished our fears
I think I'll get rich selling cheap souvenirs".

In Bournemouth and Brighton and Blackpool and Bude
the people consider the action most rude
and come the election as sure as can be
they'll vote for the party which will bring back the sea.

Also by Peter Mortimer

Poetry

Waiting for History
The Shape of Bricks
The Ooosquidal

Plays

Snow White in the Black Lagoon
The Troutbeck Time Traveller
The Man Who Played with Mice
Imagine
IT